DEADLY 60

>>>>> Factbook:
Reptiles and Amphibians
>>>>>>>>>>>

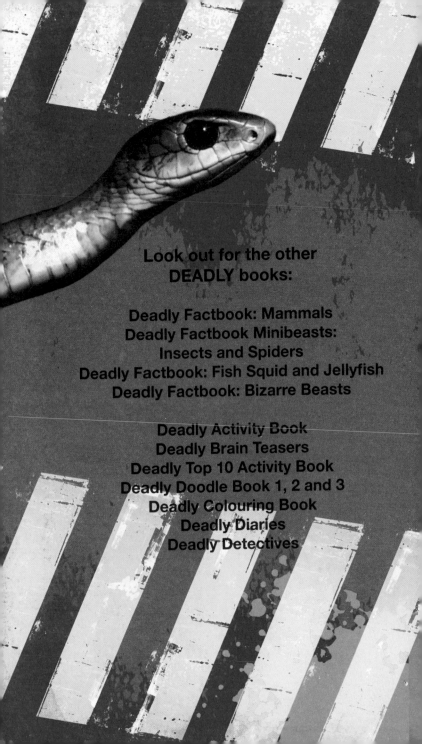

Look out for the other
DEADLY books:

Deadly Factbook: Mammals
Deadly Factbook Minibeasts:
Insects and Spiders
Deadly Factbook: Fish Squid and Jellyfish
Deadly Factbook: Bizarre Beasts

Deadly Activity Book
Deadly Brain Teasers
Deadly Top 10 Activity Book
Deadly Doodle Book 1, 2 and 3
Deadly Colouring Book
Deadly Diaries
Deadly Detectives

BBC
EARTH

DEADLY

>>>>> Factbook:
Reptiles and
Amphibians

>>>>>

Orion
Children's Books

First published in Great Britain in 2013
by Orion Children's Books
This edition first published in 2014 by Orion Children's Books
a division of the Orion Publishing Group Ltd
Orion House
5 Upper St Martin's Lane
London WC2H 9EA
An Hachette UK Company

1 3 5 7 9 10 8 6 4 2

Photo credits

1 © BBC 2009; 2 © BBC 2012; 6 © BBC 2009; 7 © BBC 2009; 11 © Jean Paul Ferrero/Ardea.com;
12 © BBC 2012; 13 © BBC 2009; 14 © BBC 2012; 15 © Ken Lucas/Ardea.com; 16 © Agephotostock/Robert
Harding; 18 © BBC 2010; 20-21 © BBC 2012; 22-23 © BBC 2010; 24-25 © BBC 2010; 26 © BBC 2009;
28 © BBC 2010; 30-31 © BBC 2012; 32 © BBC 2010; 33 © BBC 2009; 34 © Pat Morris/Ardea.com;
35 © BBC 2012; 36 © BBC 2012; 37 © BBC 2010; 38 © Andrey Zvoznikov/Ardea.com; 40 © BBC 2010;
42-43 © BBC 2009; 44-45 © BBC 2010; 46-47 © BBC 2009; 48 © Jon Cancalosi/Ardea.com; 50 © National
Geographic/Getty Images; 52 © Jon Cancalosi/Ardea.com; 55 © BBC 2012; 56 © Steve Downer/Ardea.
com; 57 © BBC 2012; 59 © Brian Bevan/Ardea.com; 60-61 © BBC 2010; 62 © BBC 2012; 66-67 © BBC
2012; 68-69 © BBC 2012; 71 © BBC 2010; 74 © Jean Paul Ferrero/Ardea.com; 76-77 © BBC 2012;
78 Stefan Myers/Ardea.com

Complied by Jinny Johnson   Designed by Sue Michniewicz

A catalogue record for this book is available from the British Library.

ISBN 978 1 4440 1259 0

Printed and bound in China

 # CONTENTS

WHAT IS A REPTILE?

A reptile is a vertebrate animal with a body covered in tough scaly or horny skin. The main types of reptile living today are turtles and tortoises, lizards and snakes, and crocodiles and alligators. There are also 2 species of tuatara, which look like lizards but are in a separate group of their own. Tuataras live in New Zealand.

Reptiles cannot control their own body temperature. They depend on the sun for warmth.

Most reptiles live on land, but turtles and a few kinds of snakes live in water. Crocodiles spend some of their time on land and some in water. To reproduce, most reptiles lay eggs that have a strong, leathery shell to protect the growing young. Some reptiles, however, such as the cottonmouth snake, give birth to live young. There are more than 8,000 species of reptile in the world today.

WHAT IS AN AMPHIBIAN?

Amphibians were the first vertebrates to live on land. Some have 4 legs, but many are limbless. There are 3 main types of amphibian: salamanders and newts, frogs and toads, and caecilians, which are legless worm-like creatures. Most amphibians spend at least part of their life in water. Like reptiles, amphibians depend on the sun for warmth.

Amphibians do have lungs but they also breathe through their skin, which must remain moist. Most amphibians lay eggs, which hatch into water-living tadpoles that grow and develop into tiny versions of their parents. Amphibian eggs have a jelly-like coating, not a shell, so they need to stay moist. There are more than 6,500 species of amphibian.

BIGGEST and SMALLEST

Chapter 1

The huge

SALTWATER CROCODILE

is the biggest of the crocodile family and
one of the world's largest reptiles.
Some can be more than 6 metres long
and weigh as much as 1,000 kilograms –
that's more than 13 people.
An average male saltwater crocodile
is about 5 metres long
and weighs 500-600 kilograms.

These crocodiles live in
northern Australia and Southeast Asia.
They swim in the sea as well as
in fresh water.

Another reptile giant is the

KOMODO DRAGON,

which is the biggest lizard in the world. The largest known Komodo dragon measured more than 3 metres long and weighed 166 kilograms. The dragons live in Indonesia, on the islands of Komodo, Rinca and Flores.

Scientists now know that this huge creature is venomous. When it bites, venom from a large gland in the lower jaw enters the prey via the wound. The dragon waits patiently for the venom to take effect, then feeds at its leisure.

The longest of
all snakes is the

RETICULATED PYTHON,

which lives in Southeast Asia.

 It grows up to 9 metres long –
that is longer than 5 tall men lying
in a line head to toe.

The
GREEN ANACONDA

of South America might
not be quite as long as the
python but it has a thicker body and can
be twice as heavy. It weighs up to 227
kilograms – more than 3 average people.
Female anacondas are the real giants and
can be up to 5 times heavier than males.

The biggest of all amphibians is the

CHINESE GIANT SALAMANDER

which grows as long as 1.8 metres from nose to tail – that's as long as a tall adult man. It lives in streams and lakes and preys on creatures such as fish, worms, insects and snails.

Most frogs are small creatures but the

GOLIATH FROG,

which lives in West African rainforests, is 32 centimetres long and weighs over 3 kilograms. Although the adults are huge, their tadpoles are only about the same size as other frog tadpoles.

The smallest frogs in the world could sit on your fingernail. The

BRAZILIAN GOLDEN FROG
and the CUBAN FROG

are both only 1cm long. But even smaller is a frog discovered in Papua New Guinea, which is only 7.7 millimetres long. It is probably the smallest of all vertebrates – animals with backbones – and could sit on a 5 pence piece with room to spare.

These little frogs are predators and catch tiny invertebrates – animals without backbones – such as mites.

GOLIATH FROG

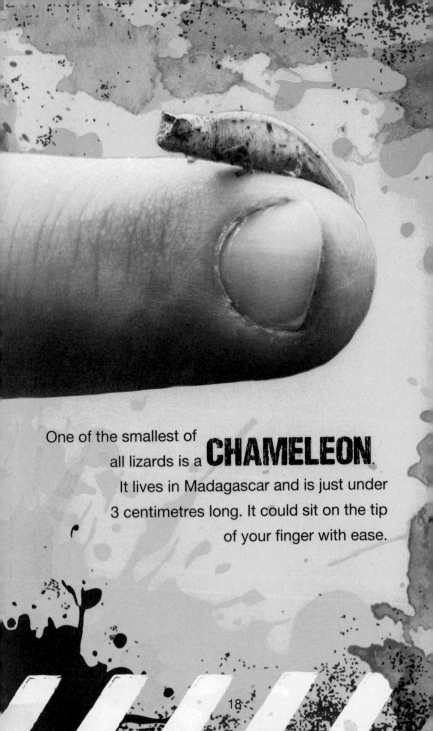

One of the smallest of all lizards is a **CHAMELEON**. It lives in Madagascar and is just under 3 centimetres long. It could sit on the tip of your finger with ease.

POISON and VENOM

DEADLY

Chapter 2

There are more than 2,700 species of snake in the world and only a few hundred of them are venomous.

The 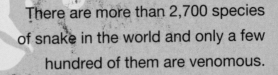 **INLAND TAIPAN** of Australia is probably the most venomous of all snakes. It uses its deadly bite to kill prey such as rats, mice and birds, but it rarely attacks humans.

 Scientists believe, though, that a single bite from a taipan contains enough venom to kill 100 people.

This snake can grow to about 2 metres long and its other common name is 'fierce snake'.

Sea snakes, such as the

BANDED SEA KRAIT,

also have very strong
venom. The snake preys
on fish and its venom needs to
be strong because a fish can
swim away after it has been bitten
and the snake would struggle to keep up.
If the venom is strong enough the fish won't get
far, and the snake doesn't lose its meal.

The female sea krait is heavier and longer
than the male. Although these snakes spend
most of their lives in the sea, the female
comes to land to lay her eggs.

Most frogs and toads have at least some
toxins produced by glands in their skin,
but the deadliest of all are the

POISON DART FROGS.

These brightly coloured little frogs live in rainforests in
Central and South America.
The poison in their skin is used as a defence,
not for killing prey, and their brilliant colours
warn any hopeful predators that they are
not at all good to eat.

The GOLDEN POISON DART FROG

has the most powerful poison and is
the most poisonous animal we know of.
These frogs are less than 5 centimetres
long, but scientists have worked out that
the skin of a single frog could contain
enough poison to kill 22,000 mice.

These frogs are called poison dart frogs because the local people use their toxic secretions on the tips of their hunting arrows.

Scientists used to believe that there were only 2 species of venomous lizard, the gila monster and the Mexican beaded lizard. They are now discovering that there are many more than they thought.

The **GILA MONSTER** is the largest lizard in North America. This creature grows to more than 50 centimetres long and preys on creatures such as birds and mice as well as other lizards.

It uses its venomous bite to defend itself though, not to kill prey.

The longest venomous snake in the world is the

KING COBRA.

Its venom is very strong and it delivers so much of it that, in theory at least, it could kill an elephant. In fact, the king cobra's favourite food is other snakes.

If threatened, this snake can raise up to a third of its body off the ground to face its enemy. It also flares the skin at the sides of its head – the hood – and makes a scary growling sound.

The king cobra grows up to 5.5 metres long – that's longer than an average family car – but most are only about 3 metres.

BIZARRE BODIES

Chapter 3

CHAMELEONS are a kind of lizard
and they catch their food with their phenomenally
long tongues.

A chameleon lies in wait, watching for prey.
When it spots a victim, it shoots out its tongue
which can be as long, or longer, than its body.
Scientists have discovered that a chameleon's
tongue works a bit like a catapult, allowing it to
shoot out at an amazing 21.6 kilometres an hour.

The prey is trapped on a sticky pad at the end of the tongue, which is then rapidly pulled back into the mouth – it doesn't have a chance.

A chameleon can change colour, but not always to hide itself, as is often thought. A chameleon may turn a darker colour if it's cold so it absorbs more warmth. A male looking for a mate turns as bright as possible to attract females. Some, such as the panther chameleon, turn red when angry.

The **EYELASH PIT VIPER** has a very special way of finding prey. It hunts at night and can 'see' warm-blooded prey in compete darkness with special heat-sensitive pits on its head. Once the snake has located its prey it makes a super-fast strike to inject its victim with venom from long fangs in the front of its mouth.

TESTING THE SNAKE'S STRIKE SPEED WITH A BALLOON OF WARM WATER.

32

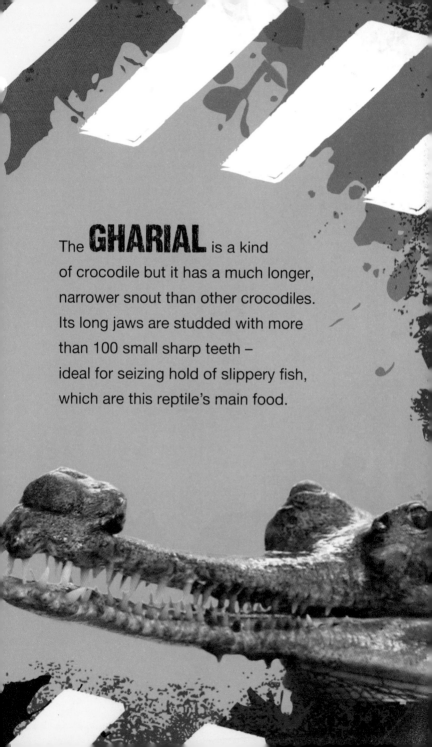

The **GHARIAL** is a kind of crocodile but it has a much longer, narrower snout than other crocodiles. Its long jaws are studded with more than 100 small sharp teeth – ideal for seizing hold of slippery fish, which are this reptile's main food.

An African snake called the **GABOON VIPER** has the longest fangs of any venomous snake. They are up to 5 centimetres – as long as an adult person's little finger.

The viper uses its fangs to inject its deadly venom into prey. It has large venom glands and produces more venom per strike than any other snake.

The buzzing rattling sound made by a

RATTLESNAKE

is a warning to its enemies – stay away from me or else. But how does the snake make this noise?

As a snake gets bigger it outgrows its skin and sheds it for a larger one. Each time the rattlesnake sheds its skin, a segment gets left behind at the tip of the tail. Once there are two or more segments, the snake can make its rattling warning. A rattlesnake may have as many as 10 segments, rarely more.

The

EASTERN DIAMONDBACK

is the largest rattlesnake and the biggest
venomous snake in North America.
It can grow up 2.4 metres long and
weigh as much 4.5 kilograms.

The **TOKAY GECKO** is a kind of lizard. At about 35 centimetres long, it is a fierce mini-predator and can crunch up beetles, moths and other insects with its strong jaws and very sharp teeth.

The secret of the gecko's success as a hunter is its climbing skill. On each toe, it has a small sharp claw that helps it grip. Even more importantly, each toe is also lined with tiny hairs that enable the gecko to cling to vertical surfaces. They act almost like Velcro to help the lizard hold on as it zooms up a wall after its prey.

The SIBERIAN SALAMANDER

is the only salamander that lives within the Arctic Circle and has a unique way of surviving temperatures as low as -35°C. The salamander's body becomes frozen and it then thaws out when the temperatures rise in spring. No other salamander hibernates in this extraordinary way.

Most creatures get bigger as
they grow older, but not the

PARADOXICAL FROG.

As a tadpole, this creature is up to
22 centimetres long, but it turns
into a frog of only about 6.5 centimetres.

The **LEAF-TAILED GECKO** is a little lizard that lives in Madagascar and preys on insects. It is a master of camouflage and is almost impossible to see as it lies on a tree trunk.

Coloured like lichen-covered bark, the gecko has a leaf-shaped tail and lots of tiny skin flaps around its body and legs. When it presses itself against the tree trunk, these little flaps flatten out and help it blend almost perfectly into its surroundings.

DEADLY HUNTERS

Chapter 4

At about 66 centimetres long, the

ALLIGATOR
SNAPPING TURTLE

is the biggest of all freshwater turtles.
It has a very special hunting device –
a little bit of extra flesh on its tongue
that acts like a lure on a fishing rod.

If a fish or frog comes near, the turtle opens
its mouth and wiggles the lure, which probably
looks very like a worm to a hungry fish.
When the fish comes closer to investigate,
the turtle snaps it up in its large beak-like jaws.

Alligator snapping turtles can weigh
100 kilograms or more. Those in captivity have
been known to live for 70 years.

BOA CONSTRICTORS

do not have a venomous bite. A boa kills its prey by wrapping its strong body around its victim and squeezing so hard that the prey animal cannot breathe and eventually suffocates.

Constricting is hard work for a snake and scientists have discovered that a boa knows just when to stop squeezing. The snake can detect the prey's heartbeat. As soon as the heartbeat stops, the boa releases its tight grip.

A boa can kill large prey such as wild pigs. Like all snakes, it cannot chew but its jaws are very flexible and can open wide enough to swallow even big prey whole. After swallowing large prey, the snake yawns to help its jaw bones resettle.

Fish are the main food of a

NILE CROCODILE

but this mighty reptile will also attack and eat more or less anything it comes across, including zebra, buffalo and other crocodiles.

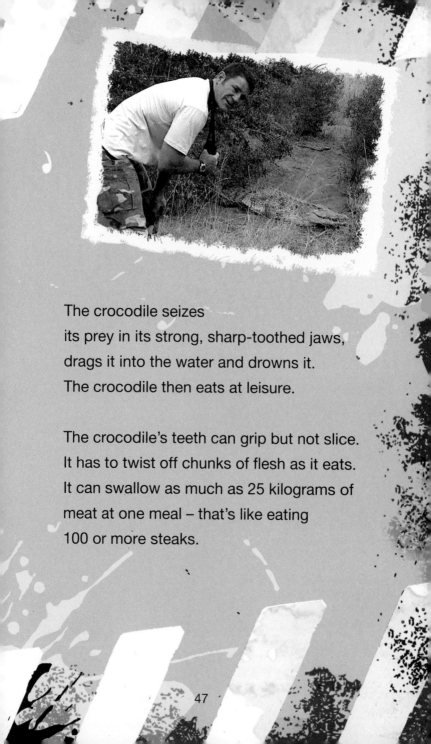

The crocodile seizes
its prey in its strong, sharp-toothed jaws,
drags it into the water and drowns it.
The crocodile then eats at leisure.

The crocodile's teeth can grip but not slice.
It has to twist off chunks of flesh as it eats.
It can swallow as much as 25 kilograms of
meat at one meal – that's like eating
100 or more steaks.

An **AMERICAN ALLIGATOR** has up to 80 teeth in its long jaws and can deliver a fearsome bite.

STAYING SAFE

Chapter 5

The **SHARP-RIBBED SALAMANDER**

has an unusual way of defending itself. If attacked, this amphibian pushes its pointed ribs through the skin on its sides to injure its enemy.

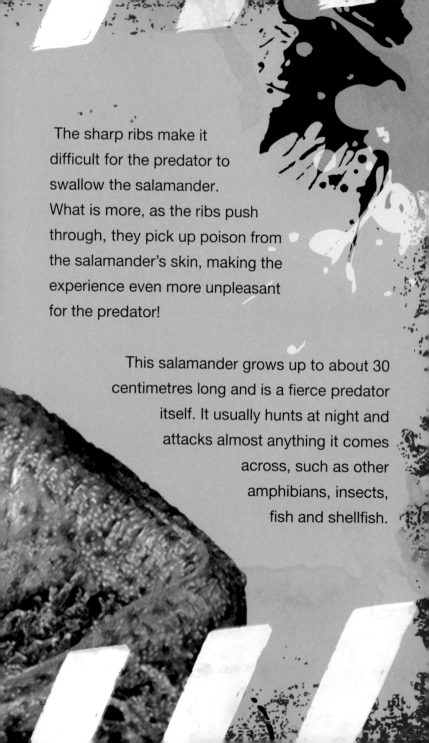

The sharp ribs make it difficult for the predator to swallow the salamander. What is more, as the ribs push through, they pick up poison from the salamander's skin, making the experience even more unpleasant for the predator!

This salamander grows up to about 30 centimetres long and is a fierce predator itself. It usually hunts at night and attacks almost anything it comes across, such as other amphibians, insects, fish and shellfish.

The **HORNED LIZARD** feeds mostly on ants and other insects which it usually hunts on the ground. If in danger, the lizard can puff up its body to twice its usual size, making it more difficult for a predator to swallow.

If the enemy doesn't give up, this lizard has another secret weapon. It squirts blood from special ducts at the corners of its eyes. It can spray this blood as far as a metre to warn off attackers.

Many lizards are able to shed their tails if seized by a predator. Incredibly, the tail may even continue to wriggle about for a short while, keeping the predator busy while the lizard escapes. The tail breaks easily at a certain point and later regrows.

A lizard can shed its tail over and over again but doing this is costly in terms of energy, particularly for those lizards that store fat in their tails.

The **SPITTING COBRA** does not need to get close to its enemies to use its venom.

Despite the name, the cobra doesn't actually spit but it can spray out venom, using muscles to contract its venom glands.

The cobra seems to be able to aim at an attacker's eyes with great accuracy. One reason for this is that the hole in the front of each fang, where the venom comes out, is smaller in the spitting cobra than in other cobras. This makes the snake's delivery of venom more accurate.

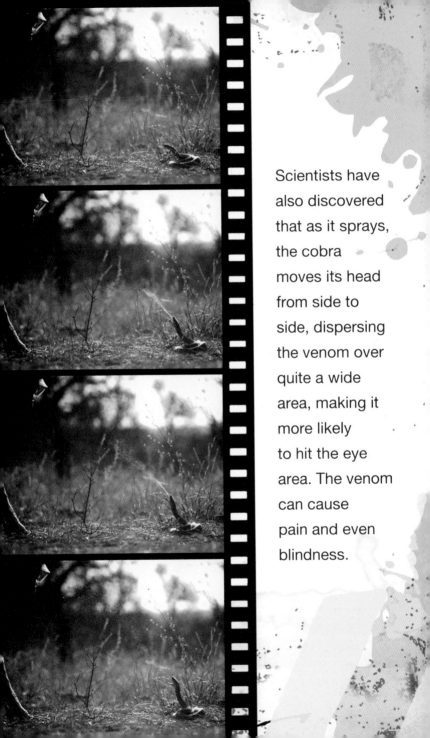

Scientists have also discovered that as it sprays, the cobra moves its head from side to side, dispersing the venom over quite a wide area, making it more likely to hit the eye area. The venom can cause pain and even blindness.

As its name suggests, the

STINKPOT TURTLE

gives off a very smelly fluid from two glands
under its shell if it feels in danger.
This turtle lives in rivers and streams
in North America.

ON THE MOVE

DEADLY

Chapter 6

There are quite a few candidates for title of fastest snake. The **BLACK MAMBA** is said to be the speediest snake in Africa and one of the fastest in the world. It moves at up to 20 kilometres an hour, but only in short bursts.

You might have heard of flying lizards and snakes, but these creatures don't really fly. However, they can glide long distances from tree to tree, which saves them going all the way down to the ground and up again.

The **DRACO LIZARD** has flaps of skin that stay folded at the sides of the body when not in use. As the draco leaps into the air, these flaps, which are supported by extra-long ribs, spread out and act like a parachute to allow the lizard to glide as far as 9 metres. The draco steers itself with its long tail.

This amazing little creature is only about 20 centimetres long, including its tail. It preys on ants and termites.

Even more extraordinary than flying lizards is a lizard that walks on water!

The **BASILISK LIZARD** can run across the surface of water for short distances. It usually does this to escape from predators such as birds of prey.

The basilisk often lies on branches overhanging water as it basks in the sun. If danger threatens, the lizard leaps down on to the water and runs so fast on its hind legs that its feet do not sink far beneath the surface, at least not at first. It is helped by its very long fringed toes that increase its contact surface area. After about 4.5 metres or so, the lizard finally sinks into the water, but luckily it can swim well!

The

SIDEWINDER

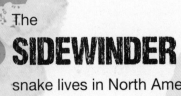

snake lives in North American
deserts and has developed a very
efficient way of moving across
hot sand. It travels sideways,
throwing its body into curves, only
a few short sections of which touch the
ground at a time. The snake pushes itself
along from these points and leaves
a trail of J-shaped tracks.

Did you know that snakes are also excellent tree climbers? The

GREEN PIT VIPER,

which lives in Southeast Asia, is an expert climber and uses its prehensile (gripping) tail to hold on to branches as it hunts in trees.

Its brilliant green colour helps it stay hidden among the leaves as it preys on lizards, frogs, birds and rodents.

FAMILY LIFE

Chapter 7

AMERICAN ALLIGATORS

are fierce predators so you might be surprised
to learn that they are also caring mums.

Once a female alligator has laid her eggs,
she covers them with plants and mud
and guards them carefully for about
2 months while they incubate.

When the eggs are ready to hatch, the young
alligators call out from inside their shells.
Their mother uncovers the eggs,
gathers any newly hatched
young in her mouth
and very gently carries
them to water. The young
stay close to their mother for
at least a year, sometimes longer.

A baby alligator is only about 15-20 centimetres long when it hatches.

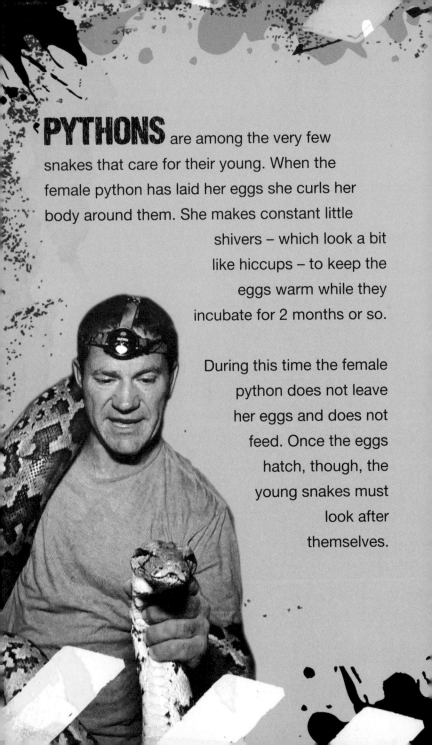

PYTHONS are among the very few snakes that care for their young. When the female python has laid her eggs she curls her body around them. She makes constant little shivers – which look a bit like hiccups – to keep the eggs warm while they incubate for 2 months or so.

During this time the female python does not leave her eggs and does not feed. Once the eggs hatch, though, the young snakes must look after themselves.

Not all snakes lay eggs.
In some, such as the

COPPERHEAD SNAKE,

the embryo develops inside the
body of the mother eventually
leading to live birth.

Some of the deadliest of all amphibians,

have good ways of protecting their own young from predators. Instead of mating and laying their eggs in water like most frogs, they mate on land. They guard their eggs and keep them moist until they are ready to hatch into tadpoles.

The tadpoles do need to live in water while they grow into frogs. The mother, or father, takes the tadpoles, 1 or 2 at a time, on her back and carries them to little pools of water that collect at the centre of plants called bromeliads.

The tadpoles can then develop in safety in these plants, which grow on the branches of trees high above the forest floor.

Their mother continues to keep them supplied with food. From time to time she visits and lays unfertilised eggs in the pools for the tadpoles to eat.

DARWIN'S FROG has an even

more unusual way of caring for its young.
Once the female has laid her eggs, the male
guards them until they are about to hatch into
tadpoles. He then picks them up in his mouth
where they settle in the vocal sac under his chin.

The eggs hatch in the sac and stay there
until they have developed into tiny froglets.
The male then spits them out into the world.

The male

MALLORCAN
MIDWIFE TOAD

also plays an important part in the care
of his young. He carries his mate's eggs
wrapped around his legs until they hatch.

FAVOURITE FOODS

DEADLY

Chapter 8

True to its name, the **THORNY DEVIL**  is covered with sharp, thorn-like spines – not a tempting meal for most predators. The lizard itself feeds on ants and is believed to eat as many as 3,000 in one meal. It catches the ants by flicking out its sticky-tipped tongue.

The thorny devil also has a cunning way of making the most of what water is available in its home in the dry Australian desert. Any drop of dew or water that lands on the devil's back is channelled along lots of tiny grooves in its body and along to its mouth.

LEATHERBACK TURTLES

are the largest of all turtles and can grow up to 2 metres long and weigh as much as 900 kilograms. These giants feed mostly on jellyfish and squid.

Like all turtles, leatherbacks don't have teeth, just scissor-like jaws, so soft-bodied creatures suit them very well.

Leatherbacks are able to dive to depths of 1,000 metres to find their prey.

KOMODO DRAGONS

are big and strong enough to tackle almost any
prey and will take creatures ranging from mice
to buffalo. They leave very little of their catch,
consuming bones, hooves and skin. A dragon
is said to be able to eat up to 80 percent of its
body weight in one sitting. That's like an average
person eating about 30 chickens in one meal.

There is only one
sea-living lizard and that is the
MARINE IGUANA.
It feeds on seaweed and dives into the water
to find its food. While feeding, the iguana
can stay underwater for as much as an hour
but has to bask in the sun afterwards
to warm itself and restore
its body temperature.